9 Ways to Leave Your Day-to-Day Operations

And Realize Your True Vision

Lloyd Thompson

9 Ways to Leave Your Day-to-Day Operations

Independently Published

Copyright © 2022, Lloyd Thompson

Published in the United States of America

220504-02091.3

ISBN: 9798356871450

For more information on 90-Minute Books including finding out how you can publish your own book, visit 90minutebooks.com or call (863) 318-0464

Here's What's Inside...

Read This First

Suppose you have been an entrepreneur for more than 45 minutes. You understand part of your magical powers as an entrepreneur is getting sh*t done.

The problem is that the more successful you become, the more stuff gets piled on your "To Do" List. Suddenly, when you least expect it, in the dead of night, your "To Do" List morphs into a "Dragon To Do" List, and you spend the rest of your days trying to slay the ever-growing-never-ending "To Do" List.

What if you could, in one fell swoop, slay the "Dragon To Do List," claim your rightful throne at the entrepreneurial round table and turn your day-to-day operations from a "Dragon To Do List" into a DOO List?

Imagine what life would be like sitting at the head of your Kingdom… err… Company, knowing your DOO is handling all of the Day-to-Day Dragons (operations of your company), and you can spend most of your time doing projects you love: strategizing company growth, creating new products, and ultimately, category domination.

Imagine the feast you'll have when all your work warriors carry you through the office halls on their shoulders to your victory celebration!

What or Who is this Magical Dragon Slaying DOO?

Your DOO (Director of Operations) is your ticket to getting back to what you loved most about your business, eliminating daily operation overwhelm, and giving you the freedom to focus on Your True Vision.

Introduction

Let me tell you the good news.

No matter your industry or business, you are not alone. We all have the same problems. Everyone struggles with team member misunderstandings, ownership of project responsibilities, implementation to completion, and systems and methodologies, all of which result in founder overwhelm, leaving you to put fires out all day.

I did tell you there was good news, right? Good news: There is a solution for every one of those problems.

There is some even better news. You don't have to implement those solutions personally! That gives you more time to focus on the "fun stuff," your true vision for the company.

Our recent client owned a global e-commerce business and was experiencing the same frustration and overwhelm many owners experience, like working 12- to 16-hour days, most of which was spent "scatter-gunning" his large team with daily tasks.

One source of constant aggravation was the feeling he was *flying blind*. No matter how hard or long he worked, he couldn't keep a handle on everything that mattered. He hated spending his energy and time on tasks he should never have been doing in the first place but was exasperated by the lack of follow-through with his team since there was no methodology for task completion.

That's where we came in. We started by implementing clear accountability and responsibility "assignments" with his team to let them take ownership of their work. We created and applied a suitable methodology for guiding his team towards meaningful goals without requiring daily "scatter-gunning." We also developed a suitable reporting mechanism so his teams could regularly share data important for business decision-making.

Best of all, we helped him leave his day-to-day operations and gave him back the freedom to focus on creating new products and spending more time "off" to reignite his passion for his company.

My hope is that you will see the real-time possibilities available to you by the time you finish reading this book. Once you escape your business's day-to-day operations, you'll be passionate about finding creative ways to focus on strategy, relationships, and shaking the tree for new business for your company. Maybe you'll finally have the time to focus on your other passions!

Whatever you decide, let this book be your guide to the **9 Ways to Leave Your Day-to-Day Operations** and begin enjoying the time and space to focus on your true vision for the company.

Lloyd

Way to Leave #1
Solving Your Team Pain Points

As your DOO "Dragon Slayer", we start by asking each team member, "What is working well? What could be improved?" If you could catch up with each team member and ask them this, you'll find there'll be one unsolved pain point that comes up again and again. Perhaps, as the owner, you didn't know about this pain point bothering your team for a while.

It's important to start here because addressing the team's pain points will help you, or your DOO, get the team on your side early on. Knowing what processes your team likes and values will tell your DOO, what they want to see more of, what processes they are happy with and things they don't want to be changed. These pain points can also form a foundation of an issues log that your DOO will regularly discuss with you.

What "Pain" Points?

I was working with a FinTech company, and they specialized in processing payments. When I joined the team, I spoke to everyone individually and quickly discovered a pain point that came up again and again. The systems used for testing the payments were nothing like the real thing.

These dodgy test systems caused project delays and costly mistakes that could have caused reputational damage if they had continued. Bringing everyone together gave the team a common voice to ask for time and money to resolve this problem. It also helped me, as the incoming DOO, win the support of each team member and our stakeholders who hadn't understood how bad the problem had gotten before the team and I came together to raise the alert and do something about it.

We do this process one-on-one. We get to know everybody, sitting down with them. Very casually, say, "Hey, what's your top pain point?" and "What's working well?"

This is great for getting the team on board because you're coming in, new, and listening to them. Solving their pain point, they think, "This person is listening to us." You've listened to their problem, but then you're going to do something about it. That's good for morale.

A DOO Solving Your Pain Points is the Beginning of the "Freedom Foundation"

As the business owner, you could do this work yourself. However, to exit a day-to-day operation, you need to bring in a DOO, and this is the perfect way to onboard them, getting them deep into the issues and helping them win the team's support. This is one way.

At this time, I also recommend that the DOO kick off an organizational audit. This will show you, the owner, where there's plenty of opportunity for improvement. This is about getting them deep into the issues early on, on something with the team to solve their problems. With all these opportunities for improvement, the DOO can start working through the biggest bang-for-the-buck items first. These are low-effort, high-impact items, the low-hanging fruit, and these have to get high priority.

Maybe the core values have been written down somewhere, but they've not been shared. This is so basic. If the company doesn't know their core values, they don't know what good looks like, and it can all be heading in different directions. Something small and simple can have such a big impact.

Now, What Do You Do?

Once we pinpoint the pain points, we'll tell the founder or CEO what we're seeing. "These are the pain points. We'll put them on a priority list and suggest this is the priority to that founder or CEO." They don't have to take that priority. We're showing them very transparently what the issues are, and if they want to adjust the priority or move something further down the list, that's fine, but at least they've seen it. They're now aware of it. It is giving them some options. If they want to do something about it, they have our recommendation. "This is what we recommend. This is where we think you're

going to get the biggest bang for your buck,"
but they have a choice.

You Keep Control

The founder and or CEO always keeps control
over whether they participate, don't, or want to
do it at a later time. It's quite often hard to hand
over the reins to somebody new. We're coming
in and giving those pain points, but letting them
know, "Hey, you don't have to do this. This is
our recommended order. If you want to move
things up and down," they have that choice.

My Encouragement to You

Ensure you've met with the team and
understood what's working well and what could
be improved. Make sure you've taken away
these things and put them into a prioritized
issue log, in which everything is prioritized by
effort and impact.

Way to Leave #2

Driving the Vision of Your Company

It is vitally important for the visionary to set forth a three-year vision for the company.

If you don't know where you're going, you're likely to end up someplace else. This is why it's important to define where you're going, not only for yourself, but so you can break this into goals and also for a DOO who can execute those goals for you.

To begin the process, ask yourself this question. How would your business look in three years if you could wave a magic wand? How would you like to interact with your business? What inputs? What outputs? Working backwards, where should you be in one year to achieve that? What are those true statements for a one-year goal? What do we need to achieve this quarter to set these yearly goals?

Chop your quarterly goals into your chosen weekly, fortnightly project rhythms. Ask your team, for every task, "Is this task aligned with getting us to our quarterly goals?" Reassess all goals, including the yearly goals, every quarter. The environment changes; therefore, updating your goals is normal. The good news is that your DOO can coach you through this and facilitate quarterly goal sessions.

Being Back in the "Visioning" Saddle

Speaking to many founders, they tell us it feels liberating for them because that's why they got into this. They started a business because they had a vision that they wanted to implement. Now they have the time to work on their vision and shake the tree for new business. That's what they wanted to do. That's where their passion sits. I think that takes them to a happier place, rather than where they didn't want to end up: focusing on daily operations. That might not be their superpower.

I think about some of the companies I've worked with, and quite often, they got into it because they had a product they were very enthusiastic about or a special skill they had that they've now turned into a business. They didn't think, "I want to run a team and keep track of goals, KPIs, and things like that." They had a vision. It puts them back where they dreamt of when they started the business.

I think it takes them to a happier place, a much healthier place. When working on your passion, you are healthier mentally, emotionally, and physically.

How Deep Is Your Vision?

If you were to wave a magic wand, what would you like it to look like in three years? Draw me a clear picture of your life and how you interact with your business.

Describe the picture fully. Visualize it. What does it look like with the team? What are they doing? How are you interacting with your team? What does that look like? What inputs are there for the team? What outputs are coming from the team? If you think about what your day looks like, can you describe that to me?

The clearer the picture, the better. That's where you can turn that very clear picture into succinct bullet points for three-year, one-year, and quarterly goals.

These goals should normally be true statements. It might say the company's revenue will be X. That could be a goal, but there might also be a goal in there, a true statement that the founder of the company is not doing daily operational activities. The owner is not involved.

There might be some level of true statements about the activities of individual people. Maybe a particular process has been handed over to somebody else. Maybe, "We've grown a new team that does the following." These can be true statements that have all come from that clear picture from the visionary or founder.

The founders and visionaries love doing this because it is one of their character traits. They are creative people. When you are asking them to be creative and paint that picture, this is normally something they're very good at and quite comfortable doing.

A Secret Vision Is Hard for the Team to Work Towards

I have one customer who had a clear vision when I asked him. The problem was that this vision wasn't written down. The team didn't know about it. The team couldn't contribute and help move the company toward these goals. We had those goals written down and published clearly on his internal website, and now everyone knows those goals and can contribute as opposed to rowing the boat all in different directions.

The goal should be structured in a true statement. It should be written as if it's come true.

"The founder is not involved in the daily operations" could be a true statement. "The annual revenue is $10 million" could be a true statement. These goals aren't set in stone forever and ever, though. The conditions and the environment change, and so should reflect the goals. We look at the three-year, one-year, and quarterly goals every quarter. The environment changes, and so, too, should the goals.

Start with the Founder First

I start with the founder first, then open up from there. The DOO starts with the founder and categorizes what they have listed. I would keep that to one side for a minute. Then I would go to the team and ask them what they think. Then, we blend the two.

We wouldn't come from the top down and say, "This is what we must achieve." We should have a view of where we want to go from the top, from the founder first, and then communicate with the team to see where they think we should go. Ideally, the result should blend the two to have the team on board. They will have a strong view and understanding of where the company should be going and implement the founder's vision.

A Goal for Your Goals

You should ensure that they have established clear three-year, one-year, and quarterly goals at the end of this piece. Those goals have been defined. They're written down and shared with everybody, and reoccurring quarterly meetings have been scheduled.

Way to Leave #3
Defining Core Values for Your Company

Before we start with Way to Leave #3, I want to point out how we are constantly touching base with the team members because, even though this is specific for allowing the founder to leave the company, at every corner and every turn, we're touching base with the team. They are key to giving you, the owner, back your freedom. As your DOO, we must get buy-in every step to ensure that everyone is rowing the boat in the same direction to give the founder that freedom.

I believe that to get the most out of people, you must ensure their interests align with what you're doing. It's the difference between saying, "Hey, I want you to get this done," as opposed to, "Hey, this is a problem we need to solve. How would you want to do it?"

Then they get the opportunity to be an artist. I think that's the difference between art and work. I can't remember who I stole the idea of art versus work from, but I think it might be Seth Godin. It was something along the lines of work, where you give something to someone and ask them to do it, whereas art is where you say, "Hey, this is the outcome I'm looking to solve."

They get to choose their adventure of how they solve it. In doing so, they're bought in. They've come up with it. It's their baby, and they're interested in solving it. I think that's why I like team members to choose their own adventures.

How Deep Do Your Core Values Run?

Your core values are your deeply held beliefs, guiding principles, or highest priorities. Does this sound like a fluffy, nice-to-have? It's important. This is the first step if you want to hire, retain, and promote the right people.

The right people are those who live your core values. You can attract and repel with core values. When you have the right core values, you can quickly see your team through a lens of who fits these values and who does not. You want the right people who live your core values getting on the bus and those who do not fit the values getting off the bus ASAP.

Your core values are a very powerful filter. Not only can you use these values as a lens to look at your people, but you can also look at these values as a lens to look at the clients you want to work with.

Let me give you an example of VirtualDOO's core values. We have four.

The first one is to *grab it and run with it*. This is about taking ownership, encouraging others, taking pride in what we do, and treating our work as art. It's also about being bold and having the confidence to speak up with your ideas and opinions.

The second one is *constant kaizen*. This is about embracing ideas and suggestions for improvement. Focus on continual incremental improvement for clients and VirtualDOO.

Then we have number three, *enablement of self and others*. We encourage, mentor, and support the client and VirtualDOO teams and enjoy learning new skills and helping others.

Finally, number four is *fun*! Our tone is casual, conversational, collaborative, and curious. We enjoy what we do with humor and connection.

Those are our examples and core values. The last core value of *fun* may sound like a joke, but this one's important.

Employees Who Enjoy Their Work Tend to Stay

My team's important to me, and I want them to enjoy what they do, and I want them to treat it like art. I want them to enjoy who they work with, which will help VirtualDOO retain my quality team.

This goal of *fun* is also a lens we use with our clients. Are we going to enjoy working with this client? If not, it's a no-go. If you don't have your core values succinctly documented and shared, work with your DOO to achieve this and share it everywhere in your business. The goal is that everyone will know what your core values are and could tell you in a heartbeat what they are. My advice is to keep to a few punchy ones that resonate with you and the goals of your business.

Your Core Values at Work

I mentioned grabbing it and running with it, and part of that is boldness. They're going to have to be bold. I want to feel that when I'm talking to someone in the interview, will they have strong confidence? Are they going to be able to challenge my ideas when I'm talking to them?

That's going to be a part of the lens I'm using when I'm hiring someone. Also, looking at my fourth core value of *fun*, when I'm talking to someone, it's not likely to be a good fit if I feel like there's no rapport or a very easy conversational interview. I will have to spend a lot of time with this person, and they will have to spend a lot of time with me. I want them to enjoy it. I want to enjoy spending time with them. That would be part of how I would use that.

I had a case not so long ago where I was hiring, and one person who ticked all the technical skills and could answer any of my questions, but I didn't feel that there was that rapport coming across. I didn't feel that there was that humor and connection. I kept on interviewing and found someone who was technically strong and had that good, fun human connection. This person's been a great addition to our team.

A friend gave me a great visual when hiring someone only based on technical skills and not including personality. "It's like talking to a paper clip. They're very functional. They get the job done, but they're not very conversational."

Using Core Values in Promoting Processes

Generally, if you were to look through the team and list the people in your team and place the core values across the top, you'd be able to see very clearly who lives these core values. You'd be able to look at the people there and see who lives those core values regularly. It's almost black and white when you look at it. If you know your team, you go, "Yep, this person does adhere to all of those," or "Nope, this person doesn't." You can use that as a part of your ongoing conversations with people. If something's gone well, you can reinforce it and say, "Hey, this thing went well. This was a great example of where you used this core value."

If something didn't go so well, we can discuss it and say, "I don't think this went so well, and I think this is because we failed on this particular core value." Another lens also comes through when we see the people adhering to the core values.

It's not the values but how they show up in terms of their technical capabilities, being a good member, the right fit for the company, and the right people we want to involve. It becomes clear that the core values will be a part of the discussion when we promote people within the company because we can say, "Look at these clear examples" regularly. It's not like we wait until the end of a quarter or something like that. We regularly use the core values in the discussion.

Some people don't take this seriously and realize how powerful it is in shaping the culture.

That culture will mean that you have people who stay for the long term and perform and work well with your team.

One of my customers did have core values. They had 10 of them listed in a document from a year before, but nobody knew what they were. Those who contributed to the original value sessions couldn't remember them because there were too many. They were also very bland and not being lived or talked about. We got this down to a few punchy ones that everyone could remember and took every opportunity where a value was used or not used and had a conversation to remind the team of the values, so we shaped the culture going forward. I often remind people, and it is brought up in conversation often.

The Sweet Spot for Core Values

I would say not more than five core values are a good number. Three to five is a nice amount because people will remember them.

There's a company in Australia called Atlassian, and one of their core values is known everywhere in Australia: Don't F the customer. It's such a powerful core value.

If you get a few punchy ones that aren't bland, then they're likely to stick.

Way to Leave #4

Designating Roles and Responsibilities

Leaving the day-to-day operations means your team, often led by a DOO, will run these operations for you. If a task lands somewhere and everyone shrugs their shoulders or points to the other person, or more than one other person ends up working on the same task, then time and energy are wasted. The team is not working well together, and this is not a team-run business. It will be difficult for you to extract yourself from day-to-day operations. You'll get sucked into deciding which person or team needs to take care of the task.

Work Out the Roles and Responsibilities

Working out the roles and responsibilities is about, one, what roles we need in the organization, and two, what responsibilities are in those roles. Your DOO can help you map this out in an org chart.

Once you have these roles mapped out, you can look at getting those right people who adhere to the core values into the right seats. Those are the roles. Being in the right seat or role is about the person, number one, getting and wanting the role, number two, and number three, having the capacity, the time, and skill to do the role.

What If the Responsibilities Are Not Documented?

Your DOO can help. After building relationships with the team, they will understand a day on the job of each member, where the work comes from, and who they interact with. This will help them establish their responsibilities.

It is important to map out the roles and responsibilities you have now and the future state you desire, so you can start thinking about who belongs in those seats when you need them.

Once you have the right people in the right seats, ensure you don't have two people in the same seat. You need to know who is accountable for what because nobody is when two people are accountable for one thing; it ends up being confusing.

This is about providing clarity and avoiding wasting time because, otherwise, work comes in, but it's unclear who does it. Two people might do it. No one might do it. Someone will point to the other person.

What I'm looking for out of this process is clear ownership and people saying, "Yeah, this is mine, and I'm going to look to improve what I do in this space because I know what my responsibilities and my accountabilities are." If that's not clear, that ownership is not strong. That draws the founder back in every single turn because things are not getting taken care of at the level they should have been, and it continues to get bumped up to the founder to solve the problem (That would be a way to never leave!). A DOO is there, so the founder never gets sucked back in.

Who Is in Charge Around Here?

When I work with clients, I see if there's an organizational chart or a listing of the team, what they do, and who reports to whom. We often have to map this chart out because who reports to whom or the responsibilities are unclear.

One client had team members reporting to not one but two managers in different teams, and these different teams did different things. This meant that team members weren't sure which work was more important as it can come from different managers. They weren't sure what their main responsibilities were. This resulted in disagreements between team members over who should be doing particular work.

This work situation brings in a lot of insecurity. Team members don't know if they're overstepping their bounds by going to a different person because they don't know who they should report to.

They don't know what their job is. If they can't clarify their job, they think, "Do I have a secure seat? What am I accountable for? What am I being measured by?" They don't know what good looks like.

As we've discussed, clarifying and rectifying the roles and responsibilities leads to increased collaboration between team members and higher task outputs as it's clear to whom the work belongs. For the business owner, it means being less involved with the team, deciding where the work belongs and who should be doing it.

Having a DOO

When you can step away from your daily operations, you have breathing room to reignite yourself and your passion. Your people are now taking ownership and are clear on what they're doing. The founder is not as involved in the day-to-day because they can see that the team knows what they need to do. The owner doesn't need to follow after everyone, ensuring they are focused on their task. The team will take ownership of it, which will allow the owner to have that extra time back so that they can get into their vision and focus on shaking the tree for new business and building relationships with new partners and businesses.

Employee Mindset vs. Owner Mindset

When people take responsibility for a project, you turn employees into a hundred different owners. An owner mentality will have your back for the company versus focusing on themselves.

It's carving out what they own for the company. This comes back to one of our core values: grab it and run with it. "Hey, this is yours. We're here to support you, but this is your thing. Own it. Take it away. If you need help, we are here to help, but this is your thing." It's important to make it clear who owns what.

There's a big disconnect because an owner mentality is worlds away from an employee mentality. If an employee has never been an owner, they lack the skills to communicate because their focus is, "What can the company give to me? What can I get from the company?" This is why having the employees and team members participate in this great mind shift is important. It's one of the easiest ways to see employees take project ownership.

Before and After

Now team members are turning away from, "What can the company give me?" They look more at, "What can I give to the company?" At the same time, being an owner or a founder who has been in their own company for 30 years, they are so far removed from an employee mentality that it is super hard for them. They wonder, "Why aren't you doing your job? This is your job. If it were me, I would do it because this is for the best of the customer and the best of the company."

That's a founder and an owner mentality of serving the customer at all costs and ensuring the company prospers to take care of their employees and customers. This is such a great bridge a DOO creates to reassure the owner, "We are going to be that bridge to turn your employees into owners."

It's all about clear ownership at its heart. Your core values and roles, and responsibilities have been documented. No two people are accountable for the same role. Does each individual fit their role? Those would be the three.

Way to Leave #5
The Magic of Methodologies

Google tells me that a methodology is a system or methods used in a particular way. I'm talking about the systems we apply to manage tasks here. What does it look like without a methodology? Here is something I've seen time and time again.

The business owner is scatter-gunning the team with tasks daily, and it doesn't feel like a plan or goal is being worked towards. Worse, the business owner is taking on more operational management as the business scales. The antidote is an appropriate system for managing tasks. This is task management methodology and a DOO to run it, so it's not you, the business owner, managing all the work.

Choosing the appropriate task management tool is not a one-size-fits-all. There are several things your DOO can do to help you. Firstly, they can work with you to improve how these tasks are delivered. What appropriate methodology needs to be installed?

If it's cookie-cutter work where tasks are the same repeatedly, perhaps *kanban* is appropriate to give transparency to the work as it flows through the pipeline. However, with projects where the tasks vary, perhaps *scrum* is the best way to plan for delivering work. Your DOO can install and run daily huddles, reviews, retrospectives, and task prioritization and refinement meetings.

Your DOO can replace you as the person delegating the tasks and train smaller teams to become self-run and run these processes for themselves. Your DOO can educate your team about good task hygiene. For example,

- Having only one assignee. If two people are accountable, nobody is.

- Due dates.

- Priorities. Is this the most important task to be working on now?

- Enough info on the ticket. This is acceptance criteria, a list of statements that will be true when the task is completed.

- Who will close the task when it is done?

- Estimates. I like simple estimates, half days or quarter days, and keeping things simple.

The beauty of using a task management methodology is that we can use this together with our goal. Way to Leave Number Two is about goals. We can ensure all of our tasks are focused on moving us closer to our quarterly goals and implementing our vision, ensuring your business is where you want it to be when you are no longer in the day-to-day operation.

Frustration and Overwhelm Story

One of my clients was experiencing the same frustration and overwhelmed many owners experienced working 12- to 16-hour days, most of which were spent scatter-gunning their large team with daily tasks.

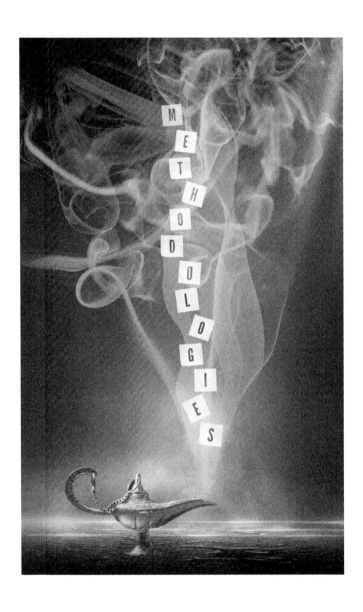

His business had multiple teams. While we could have used templates for a lot of the work, the projects being run were very customized, so we installed a scrum-like methodology for this team to run. This significantly reduced the scatter-gunning from the founder. It took them some time to get used to, but it gave the team comfort that their work would follow a rhythm. In this case, their work would be set up in two-week blocks.

Installing a methodology here meant increased happiness in the team as they could plan their work and feel like they were not living in an emergency department. For the founder, it gave him time to focus his attention elsewhere and on the company's true vision.

Whack-a-Mole

When we talk about scatter-gunning, that's negative for the founder and the employees because everybody's running in different directions. It's like whack-a-mole. We have employees trying to whack-a-mole, then someone says, "Over here! We need you over here!"

"Oh, no! Wait, wait. It's over here!"

"Nope, we've changed our minds. We scrapped that project."

That's what scatter-gunning feels like.

In the meantime, the founder is longing for that visionary role. They have many ideas for so many different people, but they don't have a systematic way of getting them from talking about it to the finish line.

Quite often, the visionaries I come across are exactly this way. They have a bazillion ideas. They are super creative, but they have trouble finishing any one thing, and they don't know any other way than scatter-gunning. They fire out, which means that people don't clearly understand what task is more important than another task. It means people aren't working well together because they haven't gone through a process. They've gone, "Well, if Fred is doing this, and Jane is doing this..." If we timed them up, so they did compatible tasks simultaneously, the work would happen much faster.

Instead, the founder is serving them all out as soon as they come out of the person's brain, which is chaos. They don't know any other way. We are educating them: "Hey, there is a way."

Part of it is putting a rhythm in place, which might involve saying, "The work is going to be set for the next two weeks. We will have a meeting to priorities what's most important, and we will set the work for the next two weeks." It's all about rhythms.

A Safe Place for Your Visionary Ideas

Having a DOO helps you have the time to create a new vision for your company and a safe place for the visionary to be able to say, "I can still have all of my ideas, and I can still throw them out there." Still, they're going to go into a safe place where we can say, "Do we want to work on this right now," or, "Okay, we want to work on it, but maybe not right now. Let's work on this next quarter."

The visionary doesn't feel like they're losing by not sharing because they still get so excited about things. Many founders are always thinking, "Oh my God! Do you know what we could do?" Then you throw that out there, and you work on it for two days, and then you get another idea because maybe you weren't quite as committed to that first one as the new one.

Having a DOO

A DOO sets the founder free to be the company visionary, allowing them to priorities. Putting them into a rhythm allows the team to see patterns and things and start taking ownership.

We are trying to look for patterns where we can eventually move the ownership from the founder to the team and have the team run as many functions as possible, so the founder's not getting sucked into everything. The founder can still have full transparency of what's happening at any time and go, "Oh, actually, we can change the priority of this one and bump it up a little bit because this one's going to be more important for right now."

A large part of it is rationalizing the chaos that's going through the founder's mind. They're still going to get what they want. They will eventually have less effort and can go through these methodologies and processes.

Besides, Whack-a-mole is very exhausting!

Way to Leave #6
Mapping Out Repeatable Processes

What does that mean? Mapping out the processes means taking what might only be in someone's head and getting it into an SOP, a standard operating procedure document.

The idea here is that you build a set of processes for how your business runs. This enables you to train new and existing staff to run your business quickly. It removes a lot of risks when key people who have a lot of knowledge leave your company.

What processes am I talking about? Let me give you a flavor: onboarding and off-boarding processes, hiring processes, HR processes for team holidays or sick leave, and accounting processes such as paying invoices or invoicing clients. I could go on. You should have processes covering everything from how a sale is made to money arriving in your account. Your DOO can work with your team to ensure that all key processes are documented.

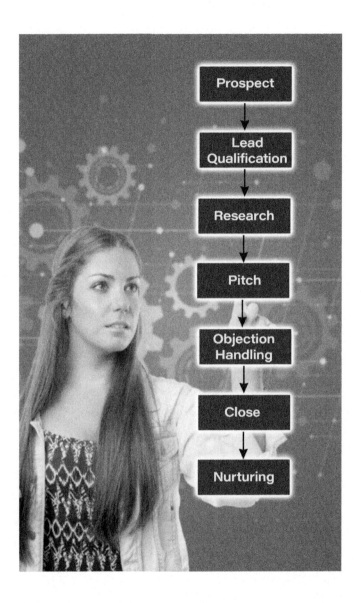

Once you have all of your current processes documented, let's optimize. Rather than tearing up the existing processes and starting again, start where you are with the existing processes. Starting with the existing processes reduces change fatigue because the team will already know the existing processes. We're not going to freak them out by tearing up their existing processes when they already have comfort in knowing what they're doing.

We have a base to work from now that these SOPs, or standard operation procedures, are documented. We can make incremental positive changes over time with the team. The Japanese call these small positive changes *kaizen*, continuous improvement. Your DOO can facilitate team sessions to improve and build on what is there already and, of course, document it into an SOP.

This is also a great opportunity to identify who is accountable for each part of the process and estimate how long each step takes. Mapping out the key processes of your business is a key step in ensuring predictability and repeatability and that your business is running smoothly.

Recipe of Analysis

One of my customers has a recipe of analysis steps that produces detailed reports for his customers. The reports were time-consuming to produce but incredibly valuable to his clients. By turning this recipe into an SOP, accompanied by a screen-recorded video of the steps, we were able to give these steps to a team of software developers who were able to automate the recipe. The lucrative recipe now runs in seconds, saving hours of his team's time. This automation has been so successful that the company owner has spun up a new agency centered on providing these automated reports. It all started with a good SOP.

Someone in their team does many things, thinking, "Oh no, what's going to happen when this person goes on a holiday or if they win the Lotto? What's going to happen here? How do I make sure that things run smoothly?" They don't know. How do they hand over that knowledge and bring it to other people in the business?

I guide them. It doesn't have to be as painful as sitting down and writing long documents. The simple way I guide them to do it is by facilitating getting some people together, the person who's imparting the knowledge and the person who is going to take on the knowledge, and do a Zoom session. One person explains to the other, "Hey, this is what it is," and shows them on the screen what's happening, how the whole process works and everything. That's the first step.

The next step is for the person who's learnt the knowledge would go away and write the SOP or a draft of it. The next time that process needs to be done, the two people will do it together. I call that "I, we, you." We've done "I."

The next time, it's "we." They do it together, and that person who's learnt the knowledge is now trying to follow the SOP that they've created from the recording, with any small changes, perfections, or refinements given by the person imparting the knowledge. If all goes well, the person who wrote the SOP now owns that going forward but can also hand that over to other people.

It doesn't have to be complex to hand over knowledge and make the processes team-run. It can be as simple as I, we, you.

Don't Let Employees Hold You Hostage

The father of a friend of mine would say, "You have to know how to do everything in your business because you can never allow your employees to keep you hostage." I think that's what happens. When there aren't repeatable processes mapped out, and you have key people hoarding knowledge, you end up making yourself vulnerable to being held hostage by your employees.

This is about reducing key-person risk in the team and not being held hostage. The end of it is like a book, but the digital equivalent of how your business runs. It might be the VirtualDOO way, where all processes of running a business could be picked up and easily handed over to new people, so I have comfort that not any particular person is instrumental and able to hold me hostage. I'm not worried about them winning the Lotto and deciding that they will leave, and my business would be in trouble.

My Encouragement to You

The very foundations of being able to leave are by having everything systematized. That's the foundation: getting everything out of people's heads. Once it's out of people's heads and outside of your head, it's easy to hand over. It means you will be less involved because it's no longer in your head. You're no longer being held hostage. You'll be less concerned about key-person risk because you can easily run your business with other new people who can join the team. You can easily ramp up and run your processes.

This is also another way to make your business sellable. If your business is you, as the founder, or the knowledge in people's heads, it's not a sellable business. Having a sellable business is having a process-run business, which is another benefit. If you want to get out of the day-to-day, you may want to leave your business and sell it eventually.

Way to Leave #7

Cashing in on Needs, Interests, and Individual Goals

You get the best out of people doing what
interests them. This increases productivity and
staff retention, meaning you don't need to hire
and train people often. This is a huge financial
saving. To realize your vision and get out of the
day-to-day operations, you need a strong,
motivated team around you to become a team-
run business.

Good people are the most important asset your
company has. This isn't an empty platitude.
How do you do this? This is about
understanding the needs, interests, and personal
goals of the individuals in the team. When your
DOO talks to each member to discover these
things, they can align the individuals' personal
goals with projects and the tasks the company
needs. In this way, when the project succeeds,
so too do the individuals who worked on the

project. In turn, this leads to increased motivation in the team.

I was put in charge of a new team, and it was clear that they were a talented bunch, but the ownership was poor. Tasks were getting palmed off to each other. There was no sense of urgency when serious issues arose. They all seemed flat.

Talking to each person, I found out what they enjoyed and what skills they wanted to develop for themselves. For some people, it was about wanting to take the lead and developing soft skills to run a team. For others, it was developing deep technical skills. I refined each person's responsibilities to get them in the right seats. Morale improved a lot. Stuff was getting done faster, and the ownership was clear. Having a happy team also meant less likelihood that anyone would leave.

What These Conversations Look Like in Real Life

A one-on-one conversation starts with, "Tell me what interests you. Paint a picture. Where do you want to go?" It's like how we started with the visionary. What does your vision look like for your business?

Start with this person painting a picture of what they'd like their career to look like in the future and mapping out the activities that interest them. I get them to list what they currently do. We can say, "What do I currently do today? What tasks do I do daily, weekly, monthly, quarterly, ad hoc?" Then I can say, "All right, highlight the ones you like doing. Then, of those things, highlight the ones you're not particularly a fan of doing."

After they do that, I'll say, "Tell me what you want to do more of?" Those are things that we can add to the list. By adding things to the list, I agree with them. If they take on these new things, they will be able to hand off those things they don't like so much. It's making a deal. It's like, "We are not expecting you to work harder for more work." We'll say, "What do you want to do more of? If you do more of that, we're keeping an understanding that you will be able to reduce some of the work and hand that over."

Of course, there's a compromise here. Some stuff needs to get done, full stop. We still need the business to run. Another one is to understand what they want. Do they want skills? "What interests you? Do you want to lead more team meetings? Do you want to take the lead in a particular project? Do you like presenting?" Then I look at the projects we have coming up and think, "Okay, maybe they can be the person who runs the team meeting, or maybe they can be the person who puts together the presentations." We're looking to align those things, and I find they get the most out of it by doing those things.

The business gets more productive outputs as well.

Clarity Creates Opportunities to Find Your Superstars

All these processes also open up a pathway to finding superstars. We often find superstars in our client companies because most people get in and do their jobs. They have that employee mentality: "I have to do my job, and then I go home," even though maybe they have insanely good ideas and they would love to run a meeting or they would love to head up their team.

Maybe they lack the confidence or the boldness to bring those ideas up. They could go the whole rest of their career there without ever bringing these ideas. You might find you have a team of superstars by talking to them about needs, interests, and individual goals. They would never be able to shine unless you went through this project process. A theme is coming up repeatedly, and that's about clarity.

More on Clarity

We don't necessarily know what's in people's heads. We're trying to get this stuff out of their heads, whether it was processes or a vision. If we don't ask about people's needs and interests, we're not psychic and will not know. We need to get that out. Quite often, there's going to be gold in there that we can go, "Oh, wow. I didn't know you had an interest in this. Perhaps we can align you more with this particular activity."

I recently discovered that someone on my team, supporting our DOO, has a keen interest in video editing. I started thinking, "Wow, there's some video editing that I can have you involved with because video editing is not something I currently have as a major talent. That will relieve some of my time and make our company's videos look better."

It's about providing clarity, getting what's in their head out on paper, and seeing if we can find a solution that works for them and the business.

It's like making money and saving money at the same time. We've realized we have a person on our team who loves video editing, so instead of having to go out and try to farm somebody we don't know, we don't like, and maybe don't even trust. All along, we're two feet from gold.

There's a sweet spot when the people you have are all part of the company's strong culture and are doing what interests them. They get into this super-motivated flow state, rowing in the same direction. That's where you want to be.

To do that, you have to get buy-in from them. You have to find out what they're interested in to take ownership and be interested in what they're doing and feel like they're achieving and not being handed work. They're accountable for something; they own something. They can choose their adventure and be an artist.

As a DOO, we fully own the gold mining for the founder.

As the DOO, we're making sure that things happen. That is done by bringing everyone together and determining their interests, needs, and goals. We're bringing them together so they all work together well to produce the best outcomes for the business.

Also, if they can get personal wins, there will be a much more productive environment. It's a huge financial saving because people will stay and grow with us for the long term.

The DOO is doing all the work of digging out the gold so that the founder can figure out what they'd like to do with all their gold.

The DOO is going to do this for the founder. The DOO can work with the team to determine the needs, interests, and goals. The founder doesn't have to do it.

Key Point to Remember

Make sure that, when a project succeeds, your people are also succeeding because you have capitalized on their needs, interests and goals.

Way to Leave #8
Setting Rules of Engagement

Setting rules of engagement means ensuring clarity about how the team should interact with each other and their leader, whether this is a DOO or you, the visionary. Time is often wasted if the team's rules aren't in place. Frustration and unhappiness build in the team, and you or your DOO will get sucked into spending time with the team. Often this is to give them clarity. How are you going to escape the day-to-day if this is often happening? Often all that is needed is to remediate some simple guidelines or rules of engagement. What decisions are each team and individual allowed to make for themselves? Do they have a financial limit? E.g., if the decision has a cost less than a thousand bucks, go for it, or if there's a sign-off process that involves a Slack channel for approvals.

One of my favorites is a rule around how disagreement or tension between members should be managed within the team. Everyone is often triggered by the perceived tone they read in an email or a text over Slack. The rule I have here is that if there's going to be a case where someone is going to disagree with someone else, they call the other person to discuss it rather than messaging them since the message does not carry the tone intended. I have found that this has reduced a lot of conflicts. However, it doesn't always work. If a disagreement persists, this is where your DOO can step in as the tie-breaker and work out the best path forward.

I have a story here. I was working with an eCommerce company, and as their new DOO, I could see that tensions were running high with each other when team members were messaging each other in a group chat, e.g., following up on each other's overdue tasks. The tone of these messages led to team members getting frustrated with each other. They were escalating to me their DOO because they were upset with each other's perceived rude comments. I brought that rule up that the team must call each other before responding in the text to anything that they perceived as negative and that they should not escalate to me unless they have first attempted to call the other person directly to resolve.

This simple rule reduced many conflicts, and it paved the way for improved relationships in the team. It also saved me their DOO a lot of time and enabled me to focus on moving the business further in the direction of the founder's vision.

A great coaching technique is when employees bring you a problem. Ask for their ideas on ways to solve it. That is a great coaching example and another way to find your superstars. I also coach like this because it's not good for them when you give them the solution they don't enjoy, especially when working with department heads. But if someone comes to you with a problem, I always believe they should come to you with a solution. I want them to at least have a go at it. It might be that one solution is to do nothing because that's a valid option. They should not just say what the options are but also choose one option because that's the difference between consulting, where you can say, "Hey, these are the options," and leading and saying, "Hey, here are the options. I put myself in this." And when you see a trend that that person is picking a good option, that you've seen work, you can zoom out further and further away and give them more and more items that you trust them with, that they can take ownership of.

Make Sure Everyone Knows the Rules of Engagement

There are clear rules about how the founder and the DOO should interact. I won't go through all of them here, but they're engagement rules like if the DOO's involved, they shouldn't go directly to the founder to seek a different role or result; that's called an end run. If part of your role is to take work away from the founder, then if someone in the DOO's team is thinking, "Well, I don't like the decision, or I don't like what's happening here." They shouldn't seek a different result by going to the founder directly because that undermines the DOO. The founder is effectively getting sucked back into the daily operations.

Anyone can talk to anyone, but there must be a clear agreement on what the founder and the DOO will do? What responsibilities sit in each person's space, and how do they engage? Normally it's simple as having a few things, like there must be a weekly meeting where the founder and the DOO come together every week to get across all of the issues and prioritize them and work together. That's one simple rule.

And another rule might be that they don't have these end runs and that people in the team shouldn't go to the founder direct for a different decision. But then there could be another rule so everyone in the business can talk to everyone. Every business will not have the same rules. We should have a rule of engagement for this. It's not about having the same rules for every business. It's about identifying what rules work for people to work together to reduce conflict, increase efficiency, and bring people to a happier place when working together.

EVERYONE Should Know How the Engagement Rules Work

Founders also need to know how to engage with their team. Sometimes, not all founders have been trained from the beginning on how to run teams or do daily operations well. Even having some simple guidelines for them that the DOO can educate them on will help. Some things might be if you're an owner and also if you are an employee, what hat are you going to wear in the business? So if you're wearing your employee hat, be an employee hat, but don't be both simultaneously. If you are the founder and you also happen to be in charge of a particular box, like finance, then you will be wearing your hat as the head of finance. You're not coming in there as an owner.

It is hard for them to do, but they need to let go of the reins and say, "Okay, if this now sits with this person, this person has that responsibility and ownership. They're in that seat. I'm going to trust them. I'm not in that seat anymore. I'm in a different seat. I'm in a different space. I'm in the founder's box and will drive out what needs to be done via my director of operations."

Way to Leave #9
Determine Reporting Cadence

Have you heard the saying, "What gets measured gets done"? It originates from Peter Drucker. You can use this simple advice in so many areas.

I was overweight. I started measuring my weight daily and changing my diet to see what worked. I'm no longer overweight. You can use this in business, too. Decide what things you want to measure and how often: sales calls, weekly revenue, customer ratings. Once you measure, you can see what actions change those measures.

However, how much data do you want to see as a business owner? Do you need to be in the weeds for every detail, or would you prefer to fly by the instrument panel of a dashboard? What data do you need to see to help you to make decisions?

It's the decision-making data that you need to get a view of regularly so that we can see what is happening in each department, an instrument panel to show that everything is going in the right direction. You might have metrics that show green when it's greater than a certain number, amber when a certain range is okay, or red for a red alert. Red needs urgent attention. Your DOO can pull this data together for you and your team and suggest what new things you should be measuring. You might want to see this data weekly, fortnightly, or monthly.

I came on board with a couple of businesses that weren't tracking the numbers that impacted their businesses. They are flying blind, and we fixed that super quick. One client knew that his sales were declining, but he didn't know his regular running costs, fixed costs, or staffing costs. This was an emergency, so we started tracking these numbers at least weekly and quickly saw what numbers we needed to achieve in the business to stay afloat. That sense of urgency around these numbers motivated the entire team to look at ways we could save money and increase sales. Within two months, my client was not only out of a financial pickle but also had his best month in 10 years.

Never Fly Blind Again

If you're letting it go, then costs you're unaware of can start to build up. One modern-day one is software costs. People buy into all tools with monthly subscriptions and are unaware that these costs are going up. Suddenly, they get hit by a huge bill, or they might not realize how much has been sitting on the credit card and will come out any day.

It can result in huge disruption for the business if people have to be let go. It could be an absolute surprise when the numbers are visible and open. It depends on if it's okay to share the numbers with the team. That's the most powerful because people start to perceive those numbers as goals, and they can work together.

They go, "Oh, wow, look how many sales we've achieved," or, "What helps us achieve that sale? What process can we go back and change? Maybe in our SOP, if we documented further, we make a few tweaks, our sales process would be better than it was before, and we'll get a few more sales going." They could say, "Oh, our customer rating's going down. There's a problem here. Maybe we need to go and tweak the process there and refine that." With our SOPs, we can go back and adjust and make small improvements, and we can then start to see where they come out in the numbers. It allows everybody in the team to work together, to achieve those goals, to get them to be green.

Cash Flow

There are simple things that people can do as well with cash flow. Sometimes even their client's cash flow is poor, but their client can pay them on credit cards. Even if their cash is slow, they're still able to pay. Then you get your money, but you can also do things like find out what the cash cycles are for your customer and align yours with theirs, so you reduce some shock.

Suddenly, you have more stable, predictable businesses where there are not so many spiky ups and downs. You're not, "Oh, no. How am I going to pay for this thing?" You're able to smooth it out.

The very act of measuring something enables you to start making refinements and improvements in your SOPs and get things to green. Otherwise, you're flying blind.

Bonus Way to Leave #10
Here's How We Can Help You

When we meet with someone for the first time, we have a short informal call to connect with you and get an understanding of your current situation. What are your top challenges and pain points? We want to know what your current team looks like. We'll ask some questions about how you are doing things today. What would be your ideal situation? How do you want it to be if you could wave your magic wand?

At the end of the meeting, we will be in a strong position to know if we can help you. We can also recommend other services or another way forward if we believe that is better suited to you.

From my side, I love meeting business owners, and it excites me to learn how we can solve their problems.

My Wish for You

Having read this book, I hope you are encouraged to take action that will lead you to escape the day-to-day operations to focus on strategy, relationships, and shaking the tree for new business, all your passions. You now know some of the key ways we can achieve this freedom or what you can ask your director of operations to take on for you.

You can contact me through my website, virtualdoo.com.

Printed in Great Britain
by Amazon

87554092R00052